BRIGHT
IDEA
BOOKS

STEPHEN
Curry

by Matt Lilley

DISCARD

CAPSTONE PRESS
a capstone imprint

Bright Ideas is published by Capstone Press, an imprint of Capstone.
1710 Roe Crest Drive
North Mankato, Minnesota 56003
www.capstonepub.com

Library of Congress Cataloging-in-Publication Data
Names: Lilley, Matt, author.
Title: Stephen Curry / By Matt Lilley.
Description: North Mankato, Minnesota : Capstone Press, [2020] | Series: Influential people | Includes bibliographical references and index. | Audience: Grades 4-6
Identifiers: LCCN 2019029512 (print) | LCCN 2019029513 (ebook) | ISBN 9781543590845 (hardcover) | ISBN 9781496665898 (paperback) | ISBN 9781543590852 (ebook)
Subjects: LCSH: Curry, Stephen, 1988—Juvenile literature. | Basketball players—United States Biography—Juvenile literature.
Classification: LCC GV884.C88 L55 2020 (print) | LCC GV884.C88 (ebook) | DDC 796.323092 [B]—dc23
LC record available at https://lccn.loc.gov/2019029512
LC ebook record available at https://lccn.loc.gov/2019029513

Image Credits
AP Images: Chuck Burton, 15, 16, Fred Jewell, 10, Jeff Chiu, 20, Ted S. Warren, cover; Icon Sportswire: Albert Pena, 19, Brian Rothmuller, 23, 25, 28, Chris Keane, 12–13, Prensa Internacional/Zuma Press, 5, 6–7; iStockphoto: Lorado, 31; Newscom: Kevin LaMarque/Reuters, 26; Shutterstock Images: Kevin Ruck, 9
Design Elements: Shutterstock Images

Editorial Credits
Editor: Charly Haley; Designer: Laura Graphenteen; Production Specialist: Colleen McLaren

All internet sites appearing in back matter were available and accurate when this book was sent to press.

Printed in the United States of America.
PA99

TABLE OF CONTENTS

CHAPTER 1

MISSING
the Shot

It was game six of the 2019 National Basketball Association (NBA) Finals. Stephen Curry was playing for the Golden State Warriors. They were playing the Toronto Raptors. The Raptors would be champions if they won this game. But Curry wanted to stop them.

Curry moved the ball past a Raptors player during the 2019 NBA Finals.

Curry was a star player. He had been picked as NBA Most Valuable Player two times. He made the most three-point shots in the NBA that year.

There were just seconds left in the game. Curry took a shot. He missed. The game was over. The Raptors won their first championship.

It hurt to lose. But Curry was proud of his team. They would keep working. They would be back next season.

Curry spoke to reporters after his team lost the 2019 championship.

CHAPTER 2

GROWING Up

Curry was born in Ohio on March 14, 1988. His full name is Wardell Stephen Curry II. But people just call him Steph. Curry grew up in North Carolina. He has always loved sports. He takes after his parents.

Curry grew up in Charlotte, North Carolina.

Curry's dad, Dell Curry (left), played for the Charlotte Hornets in the NBA.

His mom played volleyball. His dad played in the NBA. Curry practiced with the NBA players before games. But only on weekends. He had to be home on school nights.

His parents were **strict**. One day Curry did not do his chores. His mom called his basketball coach. She said he could not play that day. He remembered his chores after that.

OTHER SPORTS

Curry likes other sports too. He played football and baseball as a child.

A BETTER SHOT

Curry talked to his dad when he was 16. His dad told him to change his shot. It was too slow. The best players could block it. Curry wanted to get better. He and his dad worked all summer. He learned to shoot faster.

HIS DAD'S NUMBER

Curry wears number 30. His dad wore the same number.

Curry loved basketball from a young age.

CHAPTER 3

COLLEGE Basketball

After high school Curry wanted to play basketball in college. Some coaches did not think he was good enough. They thought he was too small.

Curry went to Davidson. It is a small college in North Carolina. The coach there saw how hard Curry worked. He did not care that Curry was small. He knew Curry could be great.

Curry became a leader on his basketball team at Davidson.

Curry cheered after his team won a game at the college tournament in 2008.

16

RECORD BREAKER

In 2008 Curry led Davidson to the college **tournament**. They played with the best teams in the country. One of the games was against Kansas State. Curry broke the record for most three-point shots in a season during that game. People in the NBA saw how good he was.

CHAPTER 4

CHAMPIONSHIP
Wins

Curry was **drafted** into the NBA in 2009. He joined the Warriors. Some people still thought he was too small. But he proved them wrong.

SHORT FOR THE NBA

Curry is 6 feet and 3 inches (190 centimeters) tall. That is shorter than most NBA players.

Curry moved to California in 2009 to play for the Warriors.

Curry held up the championship trophy in 2015. He was celebrating his team's win.

CHAMPIONSHIPS

The team won a championship in 2015 with Curry. Curry broke records. But he still wanted to do more.

In 2017 he led his team to the championship again. They played against the Cleveland Cavaliers. The Warriors had lost to the Cavaliers the year before. But this time Curry was ready. His team won.

The Warriors won another championship in 2018. It was their third one in four years.

They lost in the 2019 finals. But Curry is not done. He is still working hard today.

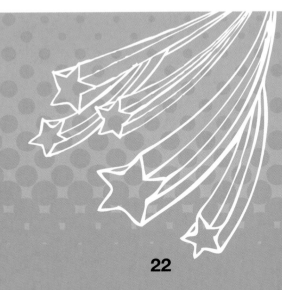

Curry high-fived teammate Kevin Durant during a 2019 game.

CHAPTER 5

HELPING
Others

Curry loves basketball. He also loves helping people. In 2017 he made 402 three-point shots. Then he gave away three mosquito nets for every shot. These nets protect people from malaria. That is an illness that people get from mosquitoes. It harms many people in Africa and around the world.

Curry is one of the NBA's best three-point shooters.

26

Curry works with former President Barack Obama. Obama started a group called My Brother's Keeper. The group works to stop **violence**. It also works with young men of color. Curry and Obama work together to help these young men.

Curry (right) and the Warriors gave Obama a team jersey.

GLOSSARY

drafted
to be selected for a team

strict
demanding that people
follow the rules

tournament
a competition that involves
teams playing several
matches of one sport

violence
a use of physical force that
hurts someone or damages
something

TIMELINE

1988: Wardell Stephen Curry II is born on March 14.

2009: Curry is drafted into the NBA by the Golden State Warriors.

2015: Curry is picked as the NBA's Most Valuable Player. The Warriors win their first NBA championship.

2017: The Warriors win another NBA championship.

2018: The Warriors win another NBA championship.

2019: Curry joins with Barack Obama to help young men of color.

2019: The Warriors lose the NBA championship to the Raptors.

ACTIVITY

PRACTICE YOUR SHOT

Curry's dad helped him practice shooting. Now Curry is one of the best three-point shooters in the NBA. You can practice shooting a basketball too. Try practicing at your school's gym or at a park with a court. You can practice with friends or a parent.

Start close to the net. Take several shots. Once you can make the shot, move farther back. When you are ready, go to the three-point line. Then try to take a three-point shot like Curry. Keep trying until you make it! Then practice until you can make the shot again and again.

FURTHER RESOURCES

Want to learn more about Stephen Curry?
Check out these resources:

Schuh, Mari. *Stephen Curry*. North Mankato, Minn.: Capstone Press, 2016.

Shea, Therese. *Stephen Curry: Basketball's MVP*. New York, NY: Enslow Publishing, 2017.

Sports Illustrated Kids: Steph Curry
https://www.sikids.com/si-kids/2016/01/12/steph-curry-sneakers-2015-season

Interested in learning more about the NBA?
Check out these resources:

Jr. NBA
https://jr.nba.com

Steele, Laura Price. *LeBron James*. North Mankato, Minn.: Capstone Press, 2020.

BRIGHT IDEA BOOKS

Stephen Curry is one of the top players in the National Basketball Association (NBA). Now he uses his fame to give back to others. Learn more about how Curry became an NBA star!

BOOKS IN THIS SERIES

LeBron James
Lupita Nyong'o
Maddie Ziegler
Michael B. Jordan
Millie Bobby Brown
Stephen Curry

capstone
capstonepub.com

$7.95 US / $9.95 CAN

ISBN
ADM
50795

9 781496 665898

JORDAN Peele

by Samantha S. Bell

INFLUENTIAL PEOPLE